Shaping My Path
From Vision to Action

Pam Ryans

Copyright © 2017 Pam Ryans

All rights reserved.

ISBN-10: 1545141673
ISBN-13: 978-1545141670

……Shaping My Path
Pam Ryans, Author
(All rights reserved by the Author, Pam Ryans)

Copyright © 2017 Pam Ryans

1 Vision Empowerment Publishing, a Division of 1 Vision Empowerment
Pam Ryans, CEO and Founder
www.1visionempowerment.com

All Rights reserved.
No parts of this book may be reproduced or transmitted in any manner whatsoever, or stored in any information storage system, without the prior written consent/permission from the publisher or the author except in the case of brief quotations with proper reference, embodied in critical articles and reviews.

ISBN-10: 1545141673
ISBN-13: 978-1545141670

Printed and Manufactured in the United States of America

FIRST PRINTING: April, 2017

ACKNOWLEDGEMENT

The completion of my book is only that, the completion of this book. However, the task of caring for young minds and doing my very best to provide information to help them succeed will forever continue.

For this particular project, I must acknowledge Dr. Bettye Mullen. It is because of her zeal for the students of the Upward Bound Program at Stillman College in Tuscaloosa that led me to place laser focus on providing excellent information for all students, regardless of academic pursuit. As a result, I owe a special debt of gratitude to Ms. Elizabeth Lowe, Ms. Wanda Holifield, Ms. Chandra Thompson, and Mr. Kendrick White for their skilled assistance.

CONTENTS

Introduction	v
Preface	vi
Section I	1
Section II	6
Section III	20
Section IV	22
Section V	28
Glossary	31
Research Resources	36
Note from the Author	37
About the Author	

INTRODUCTION

What is the one thing you love doing? What is the one thing you would enjoy doing for the rest of your life, whether you got paid or not? Think about your most enjoyable hobby, activity, or enjoyment. Now quickly think of it becoming a career. Often the activity we most enjoy is an indicator of a possible career.

This book is written to give students a glance into career options. **In this book, each shape represents a career path.** It introduces young minds to research, decision making, and developing a plan for the future.

BONUS: Optional career fair guide where students are the presenters, instead of adults.

This "Shaping My Path" chart illustrates two career choices. The student may choose to go directly from high school to the job or choose a path of obtaining additional school/training.

PREFACE

"Shaping My Path" is a follow-up from my book "When I Blow (Grow) Up, Solving the I Want to be Conversations." It was written to help children discover what they want to be when they grow up. The coloring book is centered on four different shapes, which represent students. This interactive book helps young minds with learning colors, shapes, and time management.

"Shaping My Path" will help continue the conversations most young people have with their parent(s), guardian(s), school counselor(s), relatives, or friends. It is a starting point with unlimited possibilities. This book is designed so students can begin to shape their path to success.

Questions to ask AND discuss prior to making a decision

-How far away do I want to attend school?
-Do I qualify for grants?
-Will I need a job to pay for some or all of my goals?
-Should I work while in school?
-Should I attend a 2 or 4 year school?
-How far away from home do I want to live?
-Do I want to attend a local school?
-Do I want to attend a school away from my local city/town/state?
-Are there extracurricular activities?
-Are scholarships available?
-How much does it cost to live ON CAMPUS?
-How much does it cost to live OFF CAMPUS?
-How much are houses in the area of my school or job?
-How much are apartments in the area of my school or job?
-How much is the down payment?
-Will the down payment be refunded?
-Is there local transportation?
-How much is a bus ride?
-How much is a train ride?
-How much is a taxi/cab ride?
-Will I have a car?

SECTION I

PASSION, VISION, GOALS

Often our career goal is locked inside of our passion and vision. What is your passion and vision? Maybe you already know your career goal. If you do, great! The next section lists specific jobs to help you continue your path. This is a guide to spark your interests. Listed in the research resource section are names and links to help you gain more information.

If you do not know or are unsure about career decisions, the following questions will help you come up with some ideas.

-What do you love?

If you love it, I'm sure other people love it, too. Maybe you could create a job doing what you love to do.

Ex. If you love flowers, you could own or work at a flower shop, work on a beautification committee for an organization, or become a horticulturalist, etc.

-What makes you angry?

The reason you become angry about things may be because you should create a positive solution. By coming up with a solution, you can choose a major to solve the problem.

Ex. When you go for a walk and the streets do not have sidewalks, you may become upset. Maybe you should work for the planning committee for the Department of Transportation.

-What makes you emotional?

The reason you get emotional may be because you should help heal the problem/person/animal/etc. By feeling a need to heal and help, you can major in a career centered on healing, i.e. nurse, doctor, radiologist, etc.

Ex. When you see animals that are hurting, you feel sad because you want to help. Maybe you should become a veterinarian, work in an animal shelter, etc.

-What would you do for free?

I'm quite sure you do something that you enjoy doing and without evening realizing it, you do it at no charge. BUT, to someone else it is a job. So, you could turn it into a job for yourself.

Ex. You may love writing. So, you write poems for friends and family. You could become a writer, author, poet, English teacher, etc.

-What do you notice people complain about?

People want solutions and answers to many things. You could work to solve their complaints OR create a job or product for their complaints.

Ex. Someone wanted an easier way to clean the floor, other than sweeping and mopping. So, they created a vacuum which created jobs for other people, too.

DECISION TIME

It's time to make a decision about the path you will take. Start by researching 2-3 options for your future. There are two basic options to start your research:

1. After high school graduation, do you plan on attending college immediately? Yes_____ No_____.

   OR

2. After high school graduation, do you plan to seek employment (career/job) immediately? Yes_____ No_____.

Now that you have made the first decision. Let's research:

1. Explore several career options in the next section.

2. Use your phone, computer, tablet or other electronic devices to research careers/jobs by using the links in the research resource section.

3. Visit your school or public library to research careers, and/or colleges and universities

4. Visit the college/university's website.
Suggested tabs:
-About
-Academics
-Admissions
-Enrollment
-Prospective Student

5. Find the school that has the major.

6. Find the company with the career/job.

7. Research the steps to becoming an entrepreneur.

SECTION II

EDUCATIONAL OPTIONS GUIDE (EOG)

This section list several career options based on your desired educational goals.

The **circle** represents jobs/professions that require a high school diploma.

The **triangle** represents jobs/professions that require an Associate Degree, academic certificate, or completion of a training program.

The **cube** represents jobs/professions that require a Bachelor's degree ONLY.

The **star** represents job/professions that require academic goals **higher** than a Bachelor's degree.

Career/Job Goals Requiring High School Diploma ONLY
(may include some college, but no degree earned)

The **circle** represents jobs/professions that require a high school diploma.

- Boilermakers
- Cashier
- Chemical plant and system operators
- Computer user support specialists
- Crane and tower operators
- Delivery
- Embalmers
- Hair Stylist
- Human Resources Assistant
- Library technicians
- Metal and plastic layout workers
- Metal-refining furnace operators
- Mining roof bolters
- Nursing assistants
- Occupational Therapist Aide
- Physical Therapist aide
- Production, planning, and expediting clerks
- Plastic cutters

- Press machine setters
- Retail Salesperson
- Short Order Cook
- Team assemblers
- Tractor-trailer truck drivers
- Travel Agent
- Writer

Career Goals Requiring an Associate Degree, Certification, or Completion of a Training Program

The **triangle** represents jobs/professions that require an Associate Degree, academic certificate, or completion of a training program.

- Aerospace Engineering and Operations Technician
- Air Traffic Controller
- Aircraft and Avionics Equipment Mechanics and Technicians
- Aircraft mechanics and service technicians
- Architectural and civil drafters
- Automotive service technicians and mechanics
- Bus and truck mechanics and diesel engine specialists
- Chemical Technicians
- Civil Engineering Technicians
- Computer Network Support Specialists
- Computer automated teller and office machine repairers
- Dental Hygienists
- Diagnostic Medical Sonogram Technologists and Technician
- Drafters
- Electrical and Electronics Engineering Technician
- Electro-mechanical Technicians
- Emergency medical technicians and paramedics
- Environmental Engineering Technicians
- Fitness trainers and aerobics instructors

- Funeral Service Managers
- Geological and Petroleum Technicians
- Hairdressers, hairstylists and cosmetologist
- Heating, air conditioning and refrigeration mechanics and installers
- Industrial Engineering Technicians
- Insurance sales agents
- Library technicians
- Licensed practical and licensed vocational nurses
- Massage therapists
- Mechanical Engineering Technicians
- Medical Equipment Repairers
- Medical transcriptionists
- Nuclear Medicine Technologists
- Nuclear Technicians
- Nursing aides, orderlies and attendants
- Paralegals and Legal Assistants
- Preschool teachers, except special education
- Radiation Therapist
- Radiologic and MRI Technologists
- Real estate sales agents
- Registered Nurses
- Respiratory Therapists
- Web Developers
- Welders, cutters, solders, and braziers

Career Goals Requiring Bachelor Degree

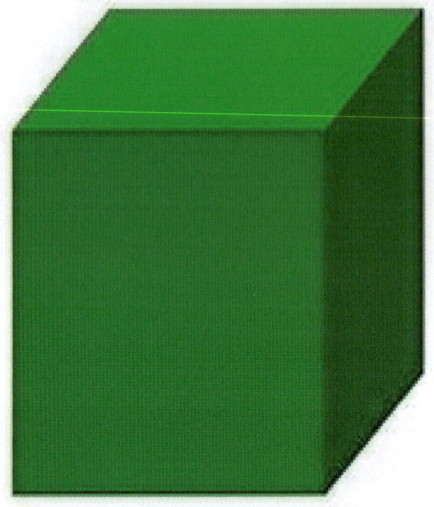

The **cube** represents jobs/professions that require a Bachelor's degree ONLY.

- Advertising Executive
- Applied Mathematician
- Biochemistry
- Biomedical Engineer
- Compliance Officer
- Computer Forensic Analyst
- Computer Programmer
- Elementary, middle, and secondary, and special education school teachers
- Engineers
- Fashion Merchandise Buyer
- Financial Analysts
- Financial Services Sales Agent
- Geoscientists
- Human Resources Specialist
- Industrial Designer
- Information Systems Manager
- Interior Designer
- Logisticians
- Market Research Analyst
- Materials Engineer
- Medical Technologists
- Multimedia Artists

- Network Systems and Data Communications Analyst
- Nurse
- Nutritionist
- Occupational health and Safety Specialists
- Production Manager
- Purchasing Manager
- Sales Manager
- Statistician
- Supply Chain Manager
- Telecommunications Engineer
- Training and Development manager
- Web Designer

Career Goals Requiring Beyond Bachelor's Degree

The **star** represents job/professions that require academic goals **higher** than a Bachelor's degree

- Aircraft pilots and flight engineers
- Archivists, curators, and museum technicians
- Biological scientists
- Chemists and materials scientists
- Counselors
- Doctors
- Editors
- Education administrators
- Environmental scientists and geoscientists
- Financial managers
- Information security analysts
- Librarians
- Logisticians, transportation, storage, and distribution managers
- Market research analysts and marketing specialists
- Marketing and sales managers
- Mathematicians, statisticians, and other miscellaneous mathematical science occupations
- Medical and health services managers
- Network and computer systems administrators
- Physician assistants
- Physicians
- Professors

- Property, real estate, and community association managers
- Psychologists
- Registered nurses
- Scientists
- Securities, commodities, and financial services sales agents
- Social, human, and community service assistants
- Social workers
- Surgeons
- Web developers

SECTION III

Research

It is very important to research the requirements of your goals. In this section are areas to conduct research and ask questions regarding your desired career/job.

If you have decided you want to begin your career/job immediately following high school, below are the areas to research:

Degree/Education Needed

    -Previous education or training needed

    -Experience Needed

    -Beginning salary

    -Benefits provided (vacation/sick time, health care coverage, etc.)

If you have decided you want to pursue a career based on the definitions in the EOG, below are the areas to research:

Community College, College, University, Professional School

-Major offered

-Program of study

-Length of time to obtain the degree

-Cost of attendance

-Application fee

-Cost of housing

-Types of financial aid available

-Graduation rate

-Location

Add additional research about the intended career to include:

-Job title

-Previous education or training needed

-Experience needed

-Beginning salary

-Benefits provided (vacation/sick time, health care coverage, etc.)

SECTION IV
From Vision To Action

The purpose of the **Vision Board** project is to assist the student with planning for his/her career. It is a visual representation of the student's passion, vision, and career/job goals.

-The Research-

-The student will gather information about the career/job from websites, newspaper articles, etc.

-The student will gather pictures from the Internet, photos, newspaper or magazines associated with the career

-The student will glue or tape on the board:

Tools Needed: Display Board, markers, color pencils, pens, glue, tape, color paper, construction paper, magazine photos, internet photos, newspaper photos.

Career/Job Goal (high school ONLY)

Choose three **top** career options. Each career option will be placed in each of the three sections on the board.

Gather or draw pictures about your career option.

Research each career option.

Include the information below for each section:

-Job Title (large letters at the top)

-Previous education or training needed

-Experience needed

-Beginning salary

-Pictures about your career

***ALSO, if you are interested in being an entrepreneur, your vision board should list start-up costs to begin the desired business.

Career Goal (BEYOND high school)

Research **two Community Colleges, Colleges, or Universities** based on your career goal.

This information will be placed on the **side** sections (left and right) of your board.

-Major

-Length of time to obtain the degree

-Cost of attendance

-Application fee

-Cost of housing

-Types of financial aid available

-Graduation rate

-Location

Gather or draw pictures about your career goal AND research your career.

This information should be placed in the **center** of your board.

-Job Title (large letters at the top)

-Degree/Education Needed

-Experience Needed

-Beginning Salary

-Pictures about your career

>***ALSO, if you are interested in being an entrepreneur, your vision board should list start-up costs to begin the desired business.

-The Board-

Career Goals

Gather or draw pictures about three career goals and glue in the follow manner.

Each Section (Right, Middle and Left)

-Job title (large letters at the top)

-Previous education or training needed

-Experience needed

-Beginning salary

-Pictures about your career

Career Goals

Gather or draw pictures about two academic goals and one career goal. Glue pictures in each section in the following manner:

Middle Section – Career Goal

-Major

-Pictures about the career

Left Side and Right Sides – Academic Goals
Choose Two Schools (Community College/ College/University)

- Length of time to obtain the degree
- Cost of attendance
- Application fee
- Cost of housing
- Types of financial aid available
- Graduation rate
- Average length of time needed in school
- Application fee
- Cost of attendance
- Cost of housing
- Types of financial aid available

SECTION V

Bonus - Career Fair

Items needed:

- Tables
- Table Cloths
- Vision Boards
- Presenters

Divide the students into 4 groups.

EACH group is made up of students who have the **SAME SHAPE**.

The Board Presentation

Option 1: Each student presents their individual board

Option 2: Students with the SAME interest present a board

Option 3: Students from each area present a board in clusters

The Verbal Presentation

- Choose presenters (choose a presenter for each board OR each section PER BOARD). Presenters are required to describe each board.

Additional Idea

Students may wear the color matching their career goal.

The **blue circle** represents jobs/professions that require a high school diploma.

The **red triangle** represents jobs/professions that require an Associate's degree, academic certificate, or completion of a training program.

The **green cube** represents jobs/professions that require a Bachelor's degree ONLY.

The **yellow star** represents job/professions that require academic goals **higher** than a Bachelor's degree

GLOSSARY

Ability

Accreditation

Advanced Diploma

Advanced Placement

Application

Associate's Degree

Association

Audit

Award Letter

Bachelor's Degree

Career

Certification

Certificate

Community College

Contract

Contractor

Course Numbers

Credit Hour

Degree Plan

Degree

Dependent Student

Direct Loan

Doctoral Degree

Educational Doctorial Degree

Externship

Extracurricular Activities

FAFSA

Fees

Financial Aid

Flat-rate Tuition

Freshman

Full-time

General Diploma

Goals

GPA

Grants

Half-time

High School Diploma

HBCU

Independent Student

Initiative

Intellectual

Internship

Interpersonal Skills

Interview

Introduction Letter

Junior

Jurist Doctorate

Loan Forgiveness

Loans

Major

Master's Degree

Minor

Non-resident

Online Courses

Part-time

Perseverance

PhD

Plan of Study

Portfolio

Prerequisite

Private University

Public University

Registration

Resident

Resume

Rolling Admission

Scholarship

Self Discipline

Semester hour

Senior

Skills

Small Business Association

Sophomore

Summer Session

Three-quarter time

Transferrable Skills

Training School

Tuition

Web Registration

Web-based Classes

Work-study Program

RESEARCH RESOURCES

The Balance
www.thebalance.com

The Best Schools
www.thebestschools.org

Handbook of Occupational Groups and Families
www.opm.gov

Small Business Handbook
www.osha.gov

Search the Occupational Outlook Handbook
www.livecareer.com

Search by topics using search engines.

Search each school's website.

NOTE FROM THE AUTHOR

I want you to know you can be successful regardless of your career goal or level. Each goal and level requires commitment, dedication, and hard work. There are great incomes on all levels for all goals. The great thing about this book is it allows you the opportunity look at a level and make a decision that will produce GREATNESS. But guess what, you're ALREADY great…to me!

ABOUT THE AUTHOR

Ms. Pamela (Pam) Ryans is a native of York, Alabama; a resident of Tuscaloosa, Alabama; and is an avid author and empowerment speaker who provide her audiences with captivating and powerful life messages.

Ms. Ryans formalized her education through attendance at Stillman College, a Historically Black College. Obtaining a Bachelor's Degree in Business Administration with a concentration in Marketing. She received a Master's Degree in Counseling and Psychology from the University of West Alabama.

She is a Best-Selling author of "Finding 'Your' Me." This book chronicles her pain, her purpose, and her passion. Unselfishly, she is the author and publisher of two other #1 Best-Selling children's books, "When I Grow (Blow) Up" (a career guide), "A Child's Tenth" (a parental guide for teaching children to tithe), "Toilet Treats", (a devotional for a private space), and Writing Your Story, The Ultimate Guide to Telling Your Story" (a writer's guide). Her books are available on Amazon and her website at www.pamryans.com.

Pam teaches writing classes in a collaborative effort with Stillman College and the University of Alabama, both in Tuscaloosa, Alabama. She hosts webinars, web-based trainings, workshops, professional training seminars, and sessions for adults and children, including one-on-one sessions.

In the midst of a diverse and vast life, Pam Ryans is the Founder of "1 Vision Empowerment," where she self-publishes and coaches other entrepreneurs. Pam provides inspirational ministry encouragement via "Transform Your Mind with Pam Ryans," text, YouTube videos, and on Facebook. Pam dedicates her personal time as a caregiver to her mother, who is a third-year, Stage IV breast cancer survivor. Through dedication for her mother, an intense desire to assist others in similar situation, and provide support for other caregivers, Pam hosts an annual event entitled, "The Daughter of Sarah." This program advocates the early detection of cancer and an awareness of the family history.

Most proudly, Pam mothers four amazing young ladies and is the grandmother of two. Her interest is expressing love through knowledge, correction, and expression. She enjoys reading, music, and just laughing at and with herself and friends.

Printed in Great Britain
by Amazon